Minimalism

Mininimalist Living, When Less is More; Value Yourself over the Material things -Practical Guide how to Declutter and Simplify your Life

Table Of Contents

Introduction 1

Chapter 1 The Minimalist Philosophy 3

Chapter 2 Being Minimalist In A Possessive Society 9

Chapter 3 How Minimalism Can Change Your Life For The
           Better 14

Chapter 4 How To Declutter Your Home 19

Chapter 5 Being Minimalist Doesn't Have To Cost More
           Money... 24

Chapter 6 How A Minimalist Lifestyle Reduces Stress 28

Chapter 7 Minimalist Tips And Tricks................................. 34

Conclusion.. 39

Introduction

Thank you for taking the time to download this book: *Minimalist Living*. This book covers the topic of minimalist living and will teach you how to simplify your life and declutter your home in order to enjoy a stress-free life. Not only that, but it will teach you how you can implement minimalist lifestyle traits even when you emerge from your home in a world that designates wealth by what you possess and own rather than by what you learn and how you act and feel.

Minimalist living is simply the practice of simplifying one's lifestyle. Whether that is getting rid of unnecessary distractions, friends, or objects within your home, this idea permeates our culture when it comes to associating relaxation and stress with our everyday lives.

Think about it: when you come home from a long day at work, you probably toss your things out of the way, kick off your shoes, flop down onto your favorite couch or chair, and you simply stare. Maybe you close your eyes and you deep-breathe, or maybe you even talk to yourself as you recount your stressful day. The point is that no lights turn on, no television is blaring, and no objects are moved near you in order to impede upon your personal space. This *is* a form of minimalism, albeit temporary minimalism.

Some people see minimalism as an increase in self-sufficiency. The decrease their independence on human-generated ideas, such as electricity, grocery stores, and even plumping, and for many this reduction in communication with the constant hustle and bombardment of humans and sounds is very relaxing and can bring a peaceful and stress-free way of life.

~ 1 ~

But, for some, this type of lifestyle is stressful to even think about.

No matter how someone chooses to exercise their minimalist lifestyle, however, there are two main components that span throughout all implementations of this form of living: the idea of being satisfied with what one has instead of dwelling on what an individual wants, and the idea of seeking inward possessions instead of outward possessions. These two ideals are what dictate some of the things we will begin to learn in this book, from how to declutter your home and make it a stress-free environment to come home to all the way to how to be minimalist on a budget.

Many people are under the incorrect assumption that being minimalist somehow takes more money. People have taken this lifestyle that is supposed to be meant for disregarding material possessions and placed within it stereotypical looks and, you guessed it, possessions to own in order to "prove" that you are minimalist. Not only will this book prove to you that being minimalist does not take a lot of money, it will show you how being minimalist goes hand-in-hand with budget living.

At the completion of this book, you will not only have a good understanding of why minimalism is a better way of life, you will also understand how to value what you learn, what you feel, and what you have to offer more than the material things you surround yourself with.

Welcome to the world of minimalist living. May the peace you find and the things you throw out not only benefit your soul, but benefit another living person.

Chapter 1

The Minimalist Philosophy

There are several spiritual and religious traditions that encourage a simpler way of living. Gautama Buddha, the biblical Nazarites (more notably, John the Baptist), and the Sramana traditions from the Iron Age in India are just a few examples of many that believe in the minimalist philosophy. Even the biblical figure Jesus is said many times in the Bible to have lived a simple life himself. He encourages his disciples within the pages of text "to take nothing for their journey except a staff -- no bread, no bag, no money in their belts -- but to wear sandals and not put on two tunics." This minimalist idea is not simply a "travel light" philosophy, like a busy salesperson traveling from state-to-state, but encompasses an entire state of being that prizes the journey over the possessions taken or purchased while on said journey.

Many other notable people in history have laid claim to the idea that spiritual inspiration had led them to adopt a simpler lifestyle and way of living: Leo Tolstoy, Mohandas Gandhi, and Benedict of Nursia are just a few of the examples that have permeated throughout history that boast of this way of living and the enlightenment and fulfillment that comes from it.

These types of minimalist living tradition span all the way back to the Orient, when it was resonating fruitfully with leaders like Zarathustra and Confucius. It was a foundational principle that was taught in the Judeo-Christian and the Greco-Roman cultures, and even a major figure within the ancient Greek philosophical practice of Cynicism, Diogenes of

Sinope, claims within the teachings that a simple life led was absolutely necessary to attain virtue.

Even today, there are many religious sects of individuals who practice a way of life that is intentionally devoid of technology and wealth, and exclude it for major philosophical and religious reasons. Some of the most popular groups are the Amish, the Mennonites, and some Quakers. The Quaker sect of the Christian belief system even has something called a *Testimony of Simplicity*, which is simply the belief that someone should life their life in a simple way, devoid of all things considered unnecessary possessions, and seek fulfillment in their lives from within and between their relationship with God.

But, there are still several individuals outside of religious and philosophical sects that regard a minimalist and simplistic lifestyle to be the way to go. Jean-Jacques Rousseau greatly praised and doted on the ways of a simple life in several of his writings. Most notably, his *Discourse on Inequality* and his *Discourse on the Arts and Sciences* base themselves around this exact principle.

A secular belief called epicureanism is based on the inherent teachings of the philosopher Epicurus. It's main principle upheld an untroubled and stress-free life and held it as the model to happiness, and taught that it could be made possible by choices that were carefully considered by an individual leading their live on a day-to-day basis. Specifically, however, Epicurus pointed out within his Athens-based teachings that troubles were brought about and constantly tripped over by harboring ideas of and maintaining and extravagant lifestyle. He taught that the extravagance usually outweighs the pleasure that is being derived from partaking in it, and this is what ultimately leads to the unhappiness within an extravagant lifestyle.

Therefore, he theorized that what is absolutely necessary for happiness and bodily comfort as well as necessary to live a basic life should be worked to be maintained at a minimal cost, and anything extravagant that requires a monetary budget to be broken should be completely avoided if it cannot be tempered by moderation.

Yet another major influencer in the minimalist lifestyle is Henry David Thoreau. This American naturalist and author is most notably known for his book *Walden*. This book is the physical manifestation of an experiment Thoreau took on for two years, where he lived life on the shores of Walden Pond and then wrote down his experiences and the lessons learned from them. He makes many statements towards advocating not simply a minimalist lifestyle, but a self-sustaining lifestyle, throughout the entire text, and is widely considered by many naturalists to be a great point-of-view into sustainable living.

But, Thoreau's influence did not stop there. In Britain at the time, Henry Stephens Salt popularized the idea of a more sane and solid style of living rooted in reality among those in his circle. Soon, other British advocates rose from the ashes to adopt this type of lifestyle and the philosophies dictated by it, and many of these advocates included William Morris, C.R. Ashbee, and John Cowper Powys.

This lifestyles trickled down within families for centuries. While the lifestyle was advocated even in the times of Jesus Christ, the religious and spiritual families passed these ideals and ways of living down through their families, and as the trend caught on in what would be considered more "modern times," England began to take hold of these ideals and passed them through the ranks as well. In the 1920s and 1930s, a family from the southern United States, the Vanderbilt Agrarians, were heavy advocators of a culture and lifestyle that was centered around sustainable and traditional values of simple farm living, and the wholly rejected the progressive and urban industrialism that was beginning to permeate throughout the nation during this time period. Many people in history, such as Richard Gregg and Thorstein Veblen, warned society against the idea of conspicuous consumption of things someone did not necessarily need, and warned heavily about the types of personality traits that could become defined and ingrained within a person because of this lavish and unnecessary materialistic consumption.

Then, people such as E. F. Schumacher came out of the woodworks and began to rally against this train of thought. As the Industrial Revolution progressed through many nations and societies, many people rallied around a "more traditional way of life" that sought to get back to simpler and more self-sustaining roots, while others voiced a way of life that meant bigger was essentially better. Those who rallied against minimalist living were garnered as heroes because they were seen fighting for progress, and those who rallied against these progressive industrialist movements were seen as traditionalists who had already "gotten theirs" and needed to sit back and let the growing generations paint the world in a way they saw fit.

That sounds a bit familiar, does it not?

What is the minimalist philosophy? Why, it is simply the conscious choice to live with less. With that broad philosophy comes many different interpretations. Some interpret it as a simply decluttering of their home every year and donating to those who are less fortunate, dubbed a "spring cleaning." Some interpret this as a lifestyle that requires selling off your home and possessions and living on a low budget while traveling the country, reducing their garbage footprint, and living life to the fullest with less, which is dubbed "motorhome living." Some interpret this as a way to completely unhook from manmade and man-generated foundational principles of living and becoming completely and wholly self-sustainable, from growing their own plants to hunting their own animals and even producing their own electricity via solar panels.

This type of living has been called "off-the-grid living."

All of these trends and lifestyles are born from one distinct idea, and that is the idea of minimalist living. Minimalism even has a trend in decorating and movie production, whereby loud colors and clutter on-screen and within the home are replaced with a monotone scale and only house the necessities in order to communicate the message or serve a basic purpose.

While that is an offshoot of minimalism, the idea of "doing more with less and being satisfied with it" still exists within those foundational creative processes and trains of thoughts.

However, living this type of lifestyle in a society that prides possessions and ownership over development of character and quality of life is a hard thing to do. Everywhere you look, people are shining their cars and purchasing their expensive sugar-laced coffee drinks while slinging their designer handbags over their shoulders and trying to avoid water puddles so they do not dirty up their newly-acquired shoes.

Remember, a minimalist lifestyle does not judge those who choose to live in excess or purchase extravagant items from time to time. A minimalist lifestyle simply chooses not to indulge in these types of practices because of a personal choice made in order to reduce the amount of stress in one's life.

So, how do you avoid all this temptation? How can you live a minimalist lifestyle without confining yourself to your newly-decluttered house that reminds you to stay on track?

It is much simpler than you think.

Chapter 2

Being Minimalist In A Possessive Society

When you step out to your car every morning, what is the first thing you think? For some, you might be wondering if your jewelry is crooked or if your makeup is smudged, or you might be running late so you are debating on whether or not to swing into your local coffee shop to grab a cup of your favorite coffee. Maybe you are wondering if your tie is crooked, or if you suit coat fits well enough and whether the look of the suit coat will have any influence on whether you acquire your dream promotion. You might be looking towards a weekend of shopping with your friends and needing that "retail" therapy in order to decompress from your stressful week.

No one stops to think that the extra hour of sleep you might have gotten instead of perfecting your makeup might have helped the exhaustion you feel. No one stops to think of how that retail therapy is going to rack of their credit card, tightening their budget for the next month, thereby creating more stress for you to muddle through. No one stops to think that there is a possibility that your boss might be looking at your job performance rather than the look of your suit coat or tie.

Now, I am not saying that a minimalist lifestyle means neglecting your appearance, never showering in order to save water for bills, and not caring about how you look to your boss. What I am saying, however, is that the emotional influence that these items have on your life is what is causing the stress and exhaustion you are feeling to begin with.

~ 9 ~

In this world, there is simply too much. There are too many shoes and too many jewelry stores, too many malls and way too many stores within those malls. Candle stores have different scents lining the square footage of their show room and furniture stores have way too many options for a budding family to choose to furnish their home with. And, with these too many products come too many sellers trying to convince you as to why you should purchase their too many products. They prey on your emotional attachment to things, convincing you that you might "need" something because of creating a false emotional connection and then feeding you a story about how they will somehow enhance the life you are living.

Then, you get home, realize you might have depleted your bank account, or dipped into your beach budget fund, or even blew your money for the electric bill, and now you are panicked, stressed, and scrambling for money.

In this world, there is too much of everything, and in many ways it is easier to live a lifestyle of "stuff" than it is to live a lifestyle of "us."

This world is busy. People bring work home with them and stay up until 1 in the morning attempting to get ahead of the game in order to make a good impression on their boss so they can forward their position in life, and in between work and promotions there are familial obligations, friendships you want to keep up if you want to have any semblance of a social life, and social media accounts beckoning for your presence if you want to keep up with modern trends and not fall behind in the world of pop culture.

In a culture of "instant," it is no wonder that shopping and purchasing physical items is the number one activity among men and women, ages 25-55.

The idea of walking into a store and walking out with something in your hand is thrilling. In a world where so much work has to be put in over a long period of time in order to acquire a minimal raise or promotion, the idea of "instant" is a nice break from that type of lifestyle. Restaurants and shopping malls alike thrive on this need for your gratification to be instant. Social media thrives on your need for instant information and instant access and instant uploads and instant on-the-second updates on your favorite celebrities.

They have preyed on your want for "instant" because the have recognized that your life is surrounded by hard work, long hours, and perseverance for something that might not even be attainable.

Then, that story rolls across our phones. Our instant-access news, 24-hour news feed throws up a story about a billionaire businessman who gave up everything he had in order to live a frugal life. And it kills us! Why would someone leave behind billions of hard-earned dollars just to live like you already do!? We regard it as almost a slap-in-the-face, that somehow living the way "average" people do after living an extravagant and rich lifestyle spits in the face of the dream *you* have, which is to work minimally and never have to worry about money again.

But, many millionaires and billionaires have done it. Jon Pedley, Percy Ross, Yu Panglin, and Chuck Feeney are just a handful of the dozens of millionaire businessmen who rose to the top, lived lavishly, drank and ate their way into million-dollar mansions on luscious beach sides, and then woke up one day and decided to give it all up for a simpler lifestyle.

They are living representations of the fact that money, goods, and materialistic things are not always the road to happiness, peace, contentment, and a good life.

They are the living representations of the antithesis of what Schumacher rallied for during the Industrial Revolution: bigger is not always better.

These men today still preach that they did the right thing. They have told many people and publications that they have found a balance in their lives that they could not find with the wealth they had, and that they could not remember a time when they had been happier.

I know, I know. You are sitting there staring at your phone screen as your rising debt screeches in the back of your mind, and you are sitting there thinking of what psychological condition they could possible have in order to justify this way of thinking. But, there is no abnormal psychological condition present, I can assure you.

So, how do you keep your minimalist spirit in a possessive society? The first step is to abide by the six major ideals of a minimalist lifestyle: less is more, eliminate the unessential, live in the moment, organize your time, find your purpose, and focus on you. By adopting and practicing these six foundational points, you will teach yourself how to turn your focus from outward motivation to inward motivation.

All around us are outward motivators: you work hard for a promotion, you stay up late at night working in order to not be fired, you diet and exercise to lose weight so you can celebrate by indulging in your favorite piece of cake. All around us are people willingly going without so they can reap the benefits of an outward motivation. This stunts many people in the area of inward motivation, where the will to do something as well as the reward both come from within. By developing ways to time manage better, you become less prone to accidents and random meetings enveloping you in stress because you have freed up time in your day to work it in. By focusing on yourself, you are able to dig deep down and find what it is you truly want instead of masking it with societal temptations in a frugal effort to achieve it now instead of work towards it for later.

By focusing on the idea of eliminating the unessential, you will prove to yourself not only how fulfilling the lifestyle can be, but you will also prove to yourself how unnecessary many of the things you purchased truly are. This can shed more light into the legitimacy of living simply than any other facet of the philosophy can.

Minimalism can change your life in ways you do not even understand.

Chapter 3

How Minimalism Can Change Your Life For The Better

A stress-free lifestyle is not the only benefit that comes from minimalism and living a simpler lifestyle free of the stranglehold of possessions. There is more to decluttering your house than no longer stubbing your toe at 3 AM when you are trying to pee, though that is a massive plus. This idea that embeds itself in the opposition of Western consumerist ideals has many different upsides that people do not realize before striking out on their own and attempting to live the lifestyle (which is wholly encouraged, by the way).

For one, less stuff means less debt, and less debt means more financial freedom. Pay down that credit card and then cut it off altogether. We are not telling you to abandon your student loans and sell off all your stuff, but what is being talked about is analyzing whether you truly need that new, expensive jacket you were going to swipe onto your credit card a few moments ago. Yes, your credit card payment might only be $15.00 a month, but with interest and credit card fees, that $100.00 jacket turns into a $150.00 jacket, and all at the expense of not having to pay the money up front.

If you only had the option of paying the money up front, would you have done it? If so, then why are you utilizing the credit card in the first place? If not, then you have not only saved yourself $100.00, but you have saved the extra $50.00 that interest and fees would have sucked from you.

~ 14 ~

Less stuff equals more financial freedom to do the things you are always dreaming of doing, like kayaking in Yellowstone or taking a vacation to Ireland.

You could even take that money and save up to purchase your own home. No one is telling you that owning a home is an unnecessary monetary purchase.

A minimalistic attitude and lifestyle can also help you help the environment. If you have less stuff, you have less to throw out or replace. This idea of constant consumerism is devastating the environment around us, so decreasing the things we have and the "necessary stuff" we use can reduce your footprint on the environment and help keep this planet that we thrive with in proper working order. With a fewer consumption of products, it means that fewer resources are necessarily expended in order to create the mounting items, and less pollution is let forth into the ecosystem.

With this minimalistic lifestyle also comes time to be more productive. If you have fewer things around you to distract you and take your time and attention, that time and attention can then be spent on things that truly matter. Whether it is spending time with friends and family or whether it is going for a walk in your favorite place to do that necessary work in a place that makes you smile, freeing your life of all those consumerist distractions can enhance the quality of life because it exchanges one source of attention for another. There are so many things you can insert into that extra time that enhance the life you are currently living -- yoga, meditation, exercising, gardening, hiking, and even fishing and hunting can all be considered stress-relieving activities that many people simply "do not have time for."

You can rid yourself of all the distractions by discarding and donating things you ultimately do not need and make the time for these types of activities that can further abate your stress levels.

Not only that, but you can rest assured that you are setting a good example for many others. If you have children, your children will watch what you are doing and learn to live their lives in the way you do. If you hate the way you spend money when you shop, but your kids are watching you do it anyway, they will pick up that habit in their latter years and struggle with the same types of things you struggle with.

But, if you can fix those struggles and lead a more stress-free lifestyle, you will teach your children that this is how life is supposed to be enjoyed.

That same influence can rub off on friends, coworkers, and even other family members like your parents. The phrase "be the change you wish to see in the world" is very true in this section of the book, because the best way to instate change in others that surround you is to emulate that change for them. Instead of talking about it, debating on doing it, and then telling others it is a good idea, simply do it yourself. Let the change in your life be the physical proof others need in order to implement the change in their own lives.

Another beautiful reason is that living a minimalist lifestyle rejuvenates your energy stores. For many people, when they step into their homes and view the clutter around them, it serves as a reminder that there are things we are letting go in our own homes. The clutter can serve as a reminder that we are constantly behind on something or having to neglect one aspect of our lives in order to focus on another. Plus, possessions have this weird power over us: they root us down in areas we do not have to be rooted in. Having too many possessions can make it almost seem like a chore to apply for that new job and move to that other state to take it simply

~ 16 ~

because we do not want to deal with the mess of clutter that exists within our homes.

So, we make our clutter and possessions the scapegoat for why we can't take that job right now that would obviously make us happier even though it pays just a little bit less.

How much life are you really missing out on because your possessions are "rooting you down?"

When you have fewer of them, you are more willing to take those risks and move, explore, and travel to areas that could ultimately result in your happiness.

However, one of the greatest possible benefits from living a minimalistic lifestyle is releasing yourself from the "comparison game." In this society, our wealth, self-worth, and social status are labeled by the things we possess. In middle school, children are ranked by the clothes they wear and whether they are name-brand clothes or not. In high school, teenagers are ranked by the type of electronics they carry around and whether it is the latest model iPhone or not. In the adult world, the comparison and ranking game is still the same.

Understand this: no one is going to stand up at your funeral one day and talk about that incredible phone you had in high school or those awesome shoes you owned in middle school. They will talk about the person you were, how you lived your life, the morals you did or did not have, and the people you did or did not love.

In the end, no one is going to remember the name of the designer that created your wedding dress. They will remember the type of person you are. When you can get yourself released from that comparison and ranking game and immerse yourself in a world where you worth is not ranked by what you possess, but by how you act and who you are, your stress levels will abate simply because you will no longer feel the need to keep on top of recent trends, fashion and otherwise. You will begin to prize what you do have instead of envying what you do not, and it will make way for the broader aspects of the minimalist philosophy to permeate the corners of your existence.

Ready for the first step?

Chapter 4

How To Declutter Your Home

For many, the first step taken in living a more minimalist lifestyle is to simply declutter their home. For some, this is the only step taken, though we encourage you to apply this type of decluttering attitude throughout your life. Many people do not understand the stress that comes with having too much stuff. Whether you are constantly stubbing your pinky toe against the leg of that chair or whether you are stressed out by all of the books and papers in your office, disorganized and unnecessary things in our lives can lead to stressors that give us the illusion we ultimately do not have control.

But, you do have control.

While decluttering your home sounds simple enough, it can quickly become an activity that is hard on anyone attempting the matter. Humans have a tendency to attach emotional sentiment to inanimate objects, whether they reflect upon our past in a positive or negative light, and this alone can prevent us from taking the steps necessary in order to relieve ourselves from the clutter that is simply in our closets, much less the clutter throughout our homes.

The first thing to do is make sure you understand the difference between preserving memories and preserving emotions. Memories, like pictures, photo albums, and sparse memorabilia are things people keep that are good. They are things that remind us of days, and people, who have passed us. Decluttering a home does not mean getting rid of these pictures and precious memories. However, there is a

~ 19 ~

difference between your child's homecoming outfit and their first crib.

One is the sheer size. The other, however, is the difference between memory attachment and emotional attachment.

Memory attachment is when you look upon an object, like a picture or that first outfit your child came home in, and you remember a physical location, face, and time it took place. An emotional attachment is when you look at an object, such as a crib, couch, or outdated piece of memorabilia and you remember the emotion behind you. You remember the moment that you first put your child in their crib. You remember those emotional times you got up at all hours of the night to come tend to your sick child. You remember the moment they finally outgrew their baby crib.

One comes with a particular moment, and another comes with a slew of moments that garner stark emotional responses.

At first, it will be hard to differentiate between the two, which is why some people sort based on sheer sizes of objects. However, this is the differentiation you are truly making: an item you keep has a tendency to be based on one particular event, whereas an item that is given away has a tendency to remind someone of multiple events.

It will come with time, do not panic.

The single greatest tip when decluttering your home is to have someone help you. They will provide an unbiased opinion when it comes to holding that leather jacket with the tag still on it that you purchased two years ago for an outing you never took. They will keep your sights set on your ultimate goal while realizing when giving away something might become too much.

The other thing to understand is that decluttering a home will not happen all in one day, and even happens in stages for many people.

Relieving ourselves of these emotional attachments is hard, and it is one of the many reasons why our "things" bring us so much stress. Being surrounded by things that constantly trigger different emotions is draining on our neuronal pathways, our limbic systems, and our adrenal glands. Being emotionally worn down is a way of life for most people, and they do not even realize it!

So, start with one room. Pick any room in your home, and make it a goal by the end of the day to have it decluttered. Bring in boxes and donate materials, or even hold a massive yard sale in order to garner some money to save back for other, more important things (like those pesky bills we all have to pay).

Then, go room by room and get rid of things that are unnecessary that you can handle parting with for now. If an item is too rooted in past emotions for you to get rid of just yet, do not panic yourself and cause yourself any more undue stress. Many people find that even decluttering their home room-by-room will take two or three different iterations before their homes are truly rid of everything cluttering it.

Just as decluttering means getting rid of things, it can also mean organizing things. Many people still utilize paperwork in order to keep records on hand for everything important they deal with when it comes to their cars, healthcare, medical bills, and important documents. While living a minimalist lifestyle can be very easy on your budget, sometimes a purchase in order to stay organized is necessary. Getting yourself a filing cabinet or hanging file folders you can place in empty pull-out cabinets is a relatively cheap investment in order to take all those important papers that are scattered everywhere and put them in a central location where you can easily reach them.

For some people, decluttering closets will come to be the hardest. Some people naturally have small wardrobes, and some people have naturally large ones. If you are someone who has a naturally large wardrobe, then here is a tip for decluttering your closet: grab a bin and set it behind you and slowly begin taking each item of clothing out, one-by-one. If you have not worn it in the past year, toss it behind your head and into the bin. These clothes can be sold or donated, and it will help you really figure out what it is you wear and what it is you simply keep around because you can.

Another way to declutter your home is to implement number-based systems. For as long as you need, you can go through your home and fill up one garbage bag of things you do not use anymore and donate or throw them away. You could also play the 12-12-12 Challenge, whereby you venture through your house and find 12 things you can throw away, 12 things you can donate, and 12 things that can be returned to their proper and correct space within the home. These number games help to switch the focus from the item to the counting correlation, which can help many people keep their emotional connections to many random items in check.

Yet another tip you can implement is to make a list. For some, the mere idea of going room to room to declutter is overwhelming. Maybe you own a larger house or have several smaller areas in your home that have served as basic storage and catch-all places. That is fine. Sit down and write out a list with every single room on it, and use it as a physical manifestation of the progress you are making. When you are done with a room, make a show of checking the room off. Scribble it out or draw over it with a thick sharpie. Find a way simple way to reward yourself by boasting of how you decluttered that room and got it in proper working order!

Decluttering your home is a massive step towards living a minimalist lifestyle, and you can have the added benefit of donating many of the items to people who are less fortunate than you might be. Consider using this time to meditate over your emotional state and allow yourself to relive these memories. Then, allow yourself to understand that the action of giving these items away does not mean you are discarding your memories. What this means it that someone can now benefit from these items and create their own beautiful memories, just like you could.

The next thing to understand is the difference between a true minimalist lifestyle and a commercialized minimalist lifestyle.

Chapter 5

Being Minimalist Doesn't Have To Cost More Money

Our society is built on the notion of bite-sized trends: tweets go viral, six-second videos get pushed to the top of "trending" charts, and two-paragraph rants on Facebook get pedaled around as recognition rains down upon their lives. As a technologically-based society, we pride ourselves in the ability to put out things that are digestible in under a minute that capture enough eyes and ears in order to consider us "viral." This temporary outpouring of love and affection is enough to boost us up because other people consider us worthy, so we find ways to keep trucking along in order to continuously build a following of people who can stroke our egos.

In other words: we have found a way to base our self-worth off tangible items that people utilize to display their lives full-frontal.

With the idea of "trending" intermingles the idea of something needing to be appealing to the eye. Things that trend usually have a visual component if the message is not verbally visceral. This means filtered photos, collage videos, and even photo and video albums garner the most attention because it engages more than one of our basic senses at a time in order to create an emotional link between the person taking in the information and the person creating it.

This means that if an idea, way of life, or principle is "trending," there is a visual aspect slapped onto it in order to convey its message without someone having to read a bunch of

~ 24 ~

text, especially if it takes more than 30 seconds to read said text.

For example, when the hygge lifestyle began to trend in the United States, multiple books were published that housed where to purchase the cheapest candles, wear to buy the best fuzzy socks, and what patterns were the most calming to put on blankets. The hygge lifestyle has absolutely nothing to do with those particular items, they are simply items that designate the hygge lifestyle in one particular culture that is born out of the Danish lifestyle that is present in their morals and weather: Denmark can be dark, very cold, and very isolating at times. So, while candles and socks to keep their feet warm are part of the hygge lifestyle for them, that same "keeping warm to be comfortable" aspect would not work to relax someone in an atmosphere such as Spain in the middle of summer.

So, when the minimalist concept began to "trend" in the United States, with it came the same visual stimulative photos with specific recurring items that people thought were necessary in order to live the lifestyle: blocked colors, baggy shirts, long monotone coats, boyfriend sweaters, baggy cardigans, and even plain leggings. People began to cast aside the meaning of "minimalism" and the life philosophy in favor of "looking the part." People began to miss the point of minimizing the trivial items and feelings in their lives and became obsessed with a "trending look" that would garner them more attention with their followers in order to continue building their "viral brand."

This is the danger of our society with principles like this, and do not fall into the trap. Minimalism, if done right, does not cost you anything. Decluttering your home does not cost anything. Downsizing your wardrobe does not cost anything.

Getting rid of some of your unnecessary furniture does not cost anything.

Why? Because you are not replacing these items. You are permanently removing them in order to make way for a simpler life with less importance on tangible items and more importance on witnessing and being present in the world around you.

For some, living a minimalist lifestyle means completely revamping how they live: many people will begin to take on this principle by decluttering their home and will find themselves so in love with the idea that they wish to sell their home or break their lease and live on the road. The most typical style of on-the-road living is known at motorhome living, but for many it can be as simple as outfitting a large van with a few basics and traveling the country.

No matter the type of lifestyle you choose to lead when it comes to your journey with minimalism, it still should never cost you much money in order to do.

For those who simply wish to get organized, decluttering does not cost anything. Then, if you have items that are important that still need a place, there are many thrift shops that house furniture and file storage cabinets for cheap when people do their own decluttering and donate. Never underestimate the bargains you can find within a thrift store if you are absolutely in need of something to help organize things that are important, like paper documents and birth certificates.

However, if you are wanting to go all-in on the minimalist lifestyle and sell off everything you own in order to work telecommute and travel across the nation, then it still does not have to take a lot of money. Scour resources you know and look for used vehicles in proper working condition. It will save you thousands of dollars purchasing used instead of walking onto a lot and purchasing something from a sales floor. Just make sure you have the knowledge to properly vet the vehicle so you are not stuck with something that will break down in two month's time.

If someone is attempting to convince you that a minimalist lifestyle somehow requires money up front, then they are missing the whole point: getting rid of possessions and unnecessary things is not only a free gesture, it is one that can save you money in the future. Many people downgrade phones and phone plans, get rid of cable and many of their streaming services, and even downgrade their homes for something a little smaller. All of these actions actually place money back into your pocket while still adhering to the philosophy of a minimalist lifestyle.

But, one of the best traits of this type of the lifestyle itself is the reduction of stress that happens within the body, and this can have massive influences over the entire trajectory of the rest of your life.

Chapter 6

How A Minimalist Lifestyle Reduces Stress

With the relief of many financial burdens comes a massive relief of stress. Whether living alone or as a group, financial issues and stressors are the number one cause of not only anxiety, but of divorce. Finances and money create stress, so being able to downsize and put money back in your pocket helps quite a bit.

But, that is not the only reason why living a simple and minimalistic lifestyle can reduce stress and anxiety.

Visual reminders are constantly impacting our state of mind. It is why "color influence" is such a popular topic in psychology today. Colors evoke specific emotions because of things we are taught as children that are ingrained into our base knowledge and neuronal pathways. So many other broader forms of knowledge are dependent upon the connections we made as children, and this is why many people associate the color red with "anger" and blue with "relief."

This is also the foundation basis of recognition, which is the idea that a visual stimulus can help someone recall an event, memory, or emotive response. However, this function never ceases to work. The things that surround you trigger emotional and physical responses every single time you visually take them in, and cluttering your life with useless things can make someone feel cramped and out-of-control. By removing those items and creating freer and more open spaces, the visual reminder transitions from a cramped sensation to an open

~ 28 ~

sensation, which can play tricks on the brain and trigger a more relaxed response.

But, with living a minimalist lifestyle comes the idea that you no longer have to keep up with trends. Stepping out of the rat-race that is brand-name products and constantly-updating technology, you free yourself from the confines of "have to have in order to be worthy." Your possessions do not define who you are. In the end, we are all buried with the same thing: ourselves. If you define yourself by your items, you will always feel as if you have to spend money that you may or may not have in order to feel like you are enough. This is a feeling of insecurity, recklessness, and competitiveness, and it can keep you in a perpetually anxious state.

Not only that, but living this type of lifestyle means you are more inclined to deal with the root causes of the issues you might have since you do not have a way to deflect and distract yourself from your problems any longer. When you are no longer always purchasing clothes for your growing wardrobe, you are able to identify the true motivation behind your constant buying: a fear of not being accepted and wanted by others.

Now, without the compulsive buying, you have to actually address the issue head-on, meaning you can truly free yourself of the stress this emotion is causing, or at least identify trigger situations that you can then avoid.

Living minimalistically also allows you to reacquaint yourself with the difference between needs versus wants. It helps you to define what is important versus what is unnecessary, and this can free up stress because you finally get in indulge in things you truly want to. You are able to care for things that hold beauty to yourself, and you are able to tailor your life to your standards and outlook rather than being a slave to possessions and the stressors that come with those possessions.

There is also an incredible self-discovery component to the entire journey. Even though you might be letting go of what you own, or some destructive habits you have taken up, it means you can focus more on yourself and what you truly enjoy and what you truly do not. When you take a good, hard look at your life without the noisy distractions of a cluttered lifestyle or mounting financial difficulties, you can finally find what makes you tick, and live your life according to your own internal clock.

This gives you a stronger sense of self, and that can instill confidence which can then help abate certain anxieties people might have when around others.

Not only that, but now that you are no longer pointlessly consuming, you have to find things you actually like. This proves more difficult for people than they might realize, because it means replacing these unhealthy coping mechanisms when you are stressed with things that are healthier. This means doing some serious self-awareness exercises in order to figure out your definition of inward health. For some, it is quiet meditation. For others, silence is terrifying, so listening to loud music while lying on the couch or bed is therapeutic.

Whatever it might be, it requires you to look. And to look within yourself, you have to have as little distractions as possible.

The truth of the matter is that a minimalistic lifestyle helps with your self-control. In this consumerist world that happened after World War II, the rise of fashion, fast food, and instant shopping catapulted us to the stressed-out, anxious society we are now. Medical issues, such as depression, diabetes, cancers, and anxiety disorders are climbing at an exponential rate, and as we continue to consume, studies show that these issues begin to climb one again on the chart of worldwide diagnoses.

Prior to this, however, people did not own as much, they did not shop as much, and they had a greater percentage of their wage in their pockets. This is not a coincidence, and it is something that can be easily remedied within an individual's lifestyle. But, stopping all of this shopping and consuming requires self-control.

By eliminating this lifestyle and assuming a minimalistic one, you are not only practicing self-control, you are abating stresses and anxieties that come with mindless purchases.

Then, after the stress has receded and the body begins to settle down and heal itself, the minimalist lifestyle brings about many different realizations. For instance, you begin to realize what truly matters. It might sound cliche, but here me out: when you begin differentiating between things you want and things you need, you start to realize just how much you thought you needed, but really didn't. This is not only enlightening, it is freeing. Eliminating what does not matter resets an individual's consumer compass, and it enables them to make better decisions with their lives going forward.

Realizing what really matters helps to keep stresses at bay that were once perpetrated by an overindulgence in consumerist ideals.

Then, you can take this idea of minimalism and apply it to your entire life. The more you focus on what matters, the easier it becomes to see the true picture. This idea of want versus need in the consumer culture can percolate and drip into other aspects of one's life, such as their dating life and their family life. Once you begin to pull back the curtain and unveil the type of person you are, with unique likes and dislikes, it becomes easier to value what is important and cast aside what is not.

For example, it might have been important to you, in your dating life, to have someone who owned their own house. But, after beginning to live a minimalist lifestyle, those priorities might shift from owning a house to being kind with children. This extension of a basic philosophy can recreate the entire lens by which we view the world, and it can set an individual's life on a track they never believed possible.

You also begin to realize that things do not make you a person. One of the biggest reasons as to why the consumer market is the biggest booming market today is because people believe that things make them who they are. Think about it: we judge someone's entire personality based on the outfit they are wearing. It's called a stereotype, and these types of things are always visually-driven. By falling prey to this ideal, we end up valuing what we see over what we experience, and we end up replacing true personalities with objects.

Many people attempt to abate their own anxieties and stressors by simply fixing the surface. Makeover shows do it all the time: they take someone with horrible fashion and makeup sense, and in thirty minutes they transform them into this instantly-beautiful version of themselves.

But, changing the surface does not abate inward stressors.

Once you get rid of all the clutter and let the minimalist philosophy percolate throughout your life choices, you will find that things do not make up who you are as a person.

You make up who you are as a person.

Living this type of lifestyle can create an incredible transformation within a person's life. It can heal them physically, mentally, and emotionally, and it can instill within them the confidence to do anything they wish. They can lead by their own compass, dictate their lives outside of traditional societal rules, and they are no longer slaves to a stressful and financially-draining consumerist lifestyle.

Even so, many people will step off the path at some point in time. This is why the minimalist lifestyle not only has a philosophy, but also tips and tricks that can aid a person in their journey from beginning to end.

Chapter 7

Minimalist Tips And Tricks

Even though a minimalist lifestyle is all about purging instead of organizing, that does not mean organization does not play a role. There are several tips and tricks to keep in mind when beginning the journey as well as things to consider while traveling the new road you have set out to travel.

There are some things to keep in mind when purging. Yes, if you have scattered papers, you might need to purchase something in order to keep them in. But, not everything needs something purchased in order to simply organize. Some people purchase organizers for their closets because they have 20 different decorative towels.

Do you really need 20?

When you consider your "reducables," make sure you know the difference between simply organizing all of your possessions and actually purging them from your home. Those seven different-sized mixing bowls might not really be necessary if you only bake during one time of the year.

Or if you bake at all.

Another thing to keep in mind is to stop bargain hunting. For many, the thrill of finding a great sale is just as much of a compulsion to purchase. Only buy what you need when you need it and you will not find yourself having to bargain hunt. This means that you will not clutter your life with useless possessions, and the possessions you do acquire will be of a high-quality, so they will last you awhile.

~ 34 ~

And, since you have saved money by living a minimalist lifestyle, the higher price still won't strap you financially.

Repurpose the time you have. Now that you have purged yourself of unnecessary possessions, you have more time on your hands. You're not cleaning or reorganizing them, so take that time and do something useful with it.

If you have a lot of stuff and do not know where to begin, start small. Living a minimalist lifestyle should relieve you of stress. So, beginning the process should not add to your stress levels. Even if starting small means, literally, tackling a corner at a time, it is more progression than you have made in months... and maybe even years.

If you are struggling to figure out whether a possession deserves a spot in your minimalist lifestyle, try to picture that item in your life a year from now. If you can't see it, then don't purchase it.

Minimalism is all about "now." Now is the time to do this, now is the time to take control of your life, and now is the time to minimize and live simply. If you pass an item in your home that you have come to feel is useless, pick it up right then and do something with it, whether you toss it in the garbage or put it in a "donation" box in your garage.

When it comes to organizing and decluttering your house, ask yourself this when tackling your kitchen: "Will it fit in a cabinet?" If not, then ask yourself how often you use it. If you have not used it at least three times in the past month, get rid of it. If you have used it but always comment on how big the item is, try selling it off or donating it and getting a size smaller. Minimalism is not about not consuming, is it about only consuming what you need.

Do not get sucked into the "trend" of minimalism: drab colors, flimsy furniture, and baggy clothes. If you want color in your life, paint your walls! If you want that nice, plush couch that you work from everyday, then get it! I will repeat: minimalist is not about "not consuming," it is about only consuming what you *need*.

Always stay on top of the decluttering. Because you have lived a consumerist lifestyle for so long, it will take mental effort in order to change the way you live. New clutter will find you for quite some time, so always stay alert for when it begins to build. Then, take the necessary steps to declutter once again. Eventually, minimalism will become the new normal in your life and clutter will find you less and less.

If you do find yourself purchasing something new, then swap it out with something old. You do not have to hold onto that rickety chair if you have purchased a better one.

Minimalism is not simply about what you do and do not keep, it is also about enriching your life. Take the money that is not being spent on goods and products and invest it into experiences and services that end up enriching your life. Have a daredevil side? Go indoor skydiving! Love to travel? Take a weekend trip to the other side of the country just to see what it's like! These types of things will also help abate anxiety and stress levels and they will provide for you enriching experiences that grow you as an individual rather than add clutter to your life.

For some, when it comes to decluttering a home organization is a massive factor. Many people do not simply have clutter, they have clutter because they are unorganized. Because of this, we have a few tips on how to help keep yourself organized as well. For starters, develop a streamlined system for something. A good start is your mail: when it comes in, have a hanging board with little baskets or boxes on them. Put the incoming mail in one box and the outgoing mail in another. Practice with this simply activity until it becomes habit, and then streamline another aspect of your life.

Disorganization, for most people, is simply the lack of implementing organizational habits.

Stop multitasking. For those who are disorganized, it can sometimes be because they are always attempting to do everyone at once. Maybe it is because of bad time-management skills, but the first thing anyone can do to tackle this issue behind disorganization is to stop multitasking: when you begin something, do not transition until it is finished or you have reached your daily goal for the project. It will be hard at first, but if you work at it diligently it will become habit.

Another way to get organized is to streamline your financial life. If you have debts and payments that are going everywhere all the time, it can become overwhelming and bills can be forgotten. If you bank with someone you trust, then consider refinancing or switching your debt payments over to the bank. Then, set up automatic debits from your account. In fact, do this with all your bills, because here is what you can do: after you set up a date and time for the auto-debit payment every month, go in and make a monthly recurring alarm on your phone without setting a terminal date.

This way, your payments will always go through on time and you will always know about them ahead of time.

If you find yourself swamped in household chores, make yourself a chore chart. Yes, it sounds like you are raising a child, but hear me out: by making a chore chart, you can easily see what needs to be done daily and what needs to be done weekly. This will minimize unnecessary cleaning moments as well as help you to organize your schedule. Don't work on Sundays? Make it your laundry day! Is your busiest day Wednesdays? Then only schedule a quick wipedown of the kitchen! It is a great way to regulate your household cleanliness around your schedule, and then once you make the schedule you never have to think about it again.

When it comes down to it, purging can harbor a lot of guilt. Maybe those crystal candleholders were expensive, or maybe your grandmother purchased you a coat that you hate, but kept because she is your grandmother and you love her. If we can let go of the guilt and other swirling emotions behind many of the items we hang on to, it will help make living a minimalistic lifestyle much easier. Items that we receive do not always have to be thrown away or tossed out in vain: consider donating them or regifting them to someone who you know would love it or could use it. In the long run, explaining to a family member why you no longer have that decoratively-mounted moose head is going to be a lot easier than constantly suffering with looking at the thing every time you walk into your home.

At the end of the day, the hardest thing to do in this lifestyle is separate the emotion from the object. No matter what we get rid of, the memories associated with that object will never leave us. Memories do not live on because the object exists, they live on because we choose to think about them with a song in our hearts.

These tips and tricks outlined above can help keep anyone in any stage of their journey on the right track, and with the help of the chapters in this book, you can be well on your way to living your own simple life that is filled with enriched adventures instead of exorbitantly rich objects.

Conclusion

When it comes to living a minimalist lifestyle, there are two main components: decluttering your life of all unnecessary possessions and disassociating yourself from the emotional attachments to inanimate objects. Humans are hardwired to attach emotion to specific things in an attempt to conjure memories because it is the easiest form of recall within the brain. Because our bodies are hardwired to work at its most efficient state, this attaching of emotion to objects that surround us is a natural occurrence.

This means that utilizing a minimalist lifestyle to the fullest extent means going against our basic instincts as a human being within a particular animalistic species.

The minimalist philosophy prides experiences that enrich an individual as a person rather than objects that give us the illusion of importance. The biggest downfall that comes from consumerism is the constant competitive atmosphere to always have the best, the brightest, and the most up-to-date technology and fashion there is. It makes someone not only a slave to society's interpretation of them, but it means they are constantly sacrificing their financial success and security in order to obtain that.

And within this dangerous and consistently-perpetuated culture, there brews a great deal of stress that is detrimental to the body as a whole.

The hormone, cortisol, is secreted when the body interprets the input of information via our senses to be a stressful scenario. This jumps the adrenal glands into overdrive, producing chemicals such as adrenaline, that mix with cortisol to enable certain types of responses: our muscles tense, our breathing increases, and our blood vessels dilate. Our bodies become primed not simply for the impact of pain, but the fight that will ensue because of that pain.

But, when activated for long periods of time, cortisol can begin to deteriorate the brain, disintegrate important muscular fibers within the body, and wreak havoc on things like the acid content within the stomach. This can lead to issues such as joint pain, lack of sleep, loss of appetite, and acid reflux disease.

When we live a minimalist lifestyle, we free ourselves from the confines of financial slavery. When we can shake off the ties and the chains that hold us to this idea that we have to paint ourselves as acceptable to society, we can regain control of our emotions, our bodily health, our finances, and we can re-center our minds in order to dig deep and promote self-awareness... and it is this self-awareness that leads to finding what we truly value in life and building a sustainable life around those moral values.

Minimalism, in its most basic form, is a return to a focus on the self. By decluttering, donating, throwing away, and reorganizing our lives, we find ways to do the same with our priorities. We find what is truly valuable within ourselves and what experiences we truly want to indulge in, and we are able to provide for ourselves a fulfilling life that leaves us with enriching experiences instead of "enriching" objects.

In a world that is as fast-paced as this one, it can be hard to find even a basic sense of peace. Many people who struggle with sleepless nights, exhaustive mornings, and even things stemming around depression and anxieties usually live high-stress lives. Minimalism can eliminate many of those stressors while simultaneously opening up your home to create massive spaces instead of always feeling as if the walls are closing in because of the sheer amount of stuff you have. With those open spaces comes an open mind and the ability to breathe better, and once the cortisol begins to dissipate from your system, the body can finally begin to physically heal.

Plus, it helps that you are not always breaking your pinky toe up against that wretched chair.

Thank you so much for taking the time to download this book. Now, you not only have an idea of what minimalism is, but you understand how it operates against society, why we are so hesitant to implement it, and how to go about implementing it even when your entire being is screaming not to. With the tips and tricks offered in this book, you should have no issues beginning this type of lifestyle, no matter the psychological and emotional issues that might be deterring you from it.

If you enjoyed this book, I would appreciate your extra time in leaving me a review on Amazon. I would love to read and digest your honest feedback because this helps me to continue producing high-quality content books for those like you who seek information.

Made in the USA
Middletown, DE
03 October 2017